ONE IS ~~NOT~~ ONE

RECONCILED AND RACIST?

Scripture quotations marked KJV are taken from the King James Version of the Bible. Public domain. | Scripture quotations marked NIV are taken from the Holy Bible, New International Version®, NIV®. Copyright © 1973, 1978, 1984, 2011 by Biblica, Inc.™ Used by permission of Zondervan. All rights reserved worldwide. www.zondervan.com. The "NIV" and "New International Version" are trademarks registered in the United States Patent and Trademark Office by Biblica, Inc.™

For foreign and subsidiary rights, contact the author.

Cover design: Sara Young

ISBN: 978-1-954089-38-9   1 2 3 4 5 6 7 8 9 10

Printed in the United States of America

ONE ~~IS NOT~~ ONE

RECONCILED AND RACIST?

DRE WILLIAMS

KUDU

CONTENTS

PROLOGUE

Warning: This book is not for the faint at heart. It contains musings that are at times hard to read along with the teaching of Scripture. My heart, as a leader, is to see God heal the racial wounds in the body of Christ.

The only way to do that is by leaders engaging in uncomfortable conversations. If we do it, the people will follow. Some of you reading about this topic for the first time will be challenged to get through parts of it. These words were written in love, the anointing, curiosity, at times anger, and a host of other emotions I'm still processing.

For others, this book will again challenge a system given to you along your journey in life. It will pull at you and shake you at your core to be a minister of reconciliation. The word "reconciliation" means "to exchange." It also means to make peace between long-standing enemies. When two people resolve their differences, we say the matter has been "reconciled."

We were enemies of God the moment sin entered the world. By His blood, we have exchanged death for life, wickedness for righteousness, dishonor for favor, and hatred for love. This is the central message of the gospel, and I emphasize its importance throughout this book. If we are truly saved—as the Bible compels us to be—it will revolutionize and inspire every decision we make and every action we take!

I encourage you to stick with reading One Is Not One until the end in order to hear the heart of Jesus. I write first to leaders in God's vineyard in America who are white and black. It is our moment in history to challenge the deception and division in the church that have made us enemies for decades.

I also write to every other ethnic group in our country and world that longs to see the Day of Pentecost unity we read about in Acts of the Apostles, Chapter 2. It is time for the nations within the church to unite and be the light and witness Jesus prayed we would be in these last days.

This book is a call to action. Nothing more. Nothing less. I'm convinced that race relations in our world could improve greatly if the church would lead the charge. We've lacked results in this area for decades. I want to do my part to turn this horror around. There are three things, I believe, that no human can hold against another human:

1) The way a person feels about something emotionally
2) The way a person's behavior has impacted another person and
3) The experiences a person has gone through.

In this book, I talk about all three. Go there with me. Some of this conversation will be painful and some pleasant. All will be helpful.

In *One Is Not One*, we'll look at the prophetic prayer of Jesus in John 17 and how this prayer applies to our day. I highlight John 17:21 to question if we are truly "one" as Jesus prayed we would be or if racism and division are hindering this prayer from being answered.

Please pray before you read this book. Pray for a reconciled mind. Let this book inspire you. Allow what you are about to read to thrust you into movement.

This book was written to be used in small group discussions and to create dialogue. I also want to see Sunday messages, panel discussions, Bible classes, podcast episodes, and one-on-one conversations centered around this message of reconciliation.

At the end of each chapter there are group discussion questions that are sure to provoke the sharing of emotions, stories, and experiences. Additionally, I have added pages for journaling. Document at least one thing from each chapter that challenged or impacted you. Track the progress of your actions. Record new experiences filled with the love of Christ.

Share your thoughts in your group. Small groups can be life-changing. Please be open. If small groups aren't your thing, use the extra pages at the end of each chapter to jot down your answers and journal personal questions or thoughts that come to mind.

I also invite the nations to join this conversation. I exclude no one whom Jesus has purchased. We need to hear your voice, so please don't turn away because you're not religious. Let's seek to learn from one another.

Please consider the maturity level of the person you sit across from and allow mistakes to be made. We will only fix this problem by talking and changing our ways.

The only way to do better is to do better.

This book is dedicated to my grandfather Minister Earnest Greenlee. Thank you for your leadership, love, hugs, and for your example. We miss you. Until we meet again.

CHAPTER 1

UPLIFTED EYES

I believe that if there were anyone who could get what they ask for every time in prayer, it would be Jesus. As we take a look at this monumental prayer of the Son of God in John 17, I want to make correlations to where we are now and where we have been.

In John 17:1, shortly before suffering betrayal and crucifixion, we see the precious Lamb of God making His final preparations to be willingly led to the slaughter for all humanity. He prays, "Father, the hour has come. Glorify your Son, that your Son may glorify you" (NIV).

In his "Cornerstone Speech" on March 21, 1861, Confederate Vice President Alexander H. Stephens vehemently denied the Creator's universal love for His creation. He said, and I quote, "Our new government is founded upon exactly the opposite ideas [as the Union's government];

its foundations are laid, its cornerstone rests, upon the great truth that the negro is not equal to the white man; that slavery, subordination to the superior race, is his natural and normal condition."

He went on to describe a conversation he had with a gentleman from the Northern states who asserted that the South would have to eventually give up slavery. Stephens argued back that the North would ultimately fail. "The truth announced, that it was as impossible to war success-fully against a principle in politics as it was in physics and mechanics, I admitted; but told him that it was he, and those acting with him, who were warring against a principle. They were attempting to make things equal which the Creator had made unequal."

Filled with racial hostility and arrogance, he sought to keep a people enslaved who had been set free before freedom was told to soar on its wings of justice.

America has always contradicted its story of freedom for all by its unwillingness to place ample amounts of respect on the names of the Africans in America. If we are to ever secure a right religion, we must openly respect that Jesus in His pre-walk to Calvary, lifted up His eyes to a perfect God who loves everyone.

If your mind won't allow you to accept this divine fact, your religion is worthless. Mr. Alexander confidently presented a unilateral message to white Americans—rich and poor alike—that theirs were the only souls God cared for. Law was their equal reward. He discredited the North's view of equality and freedom from the evils of slavery and viewed its position as just as inferior as the blacks he sought to shut down "forever."

What a frightening mindset. To take the divine word of God Almighty and manipulate an entire nation. I wonder if many of those slave owners, racist lawmakers, and bigoted politicians ever took the time to prayerfully read—by the Spirit—John 17. I wonder if God's Word revealed to these men their own deception and pride. I know for sure that any mind that approaches it without the distractions of preconceived notions and biases will—without prejudice—see a Man strapped with the burden of not only a sinful generation but also a sinful creation.

In a prophetic position that none other before or after would ever attain, Our Lord took His eyes of fire and directed them towards His eternal Father for the purpose of intercession. Friend, if our Savior was compelled to look upward, what about you? What makes you look around in terror at the racial tensions and hostilities we are all becoming desensitized to?

LOST PREVENTION

As with any company that seeks to protect its assets, it employs a loss prevention team to tackle the root causes of any financial losses sustained in its profit and loss statement. These companies hire shrewd and brilliant minds to mitigate any losses and to readily investigate potential losses. It requires keen insight and discipline to get to the bottom of problems that can wreak havoc on a business.

I want to shift from "loss prevention" to "lost prevention." With as much discipline as it takes to protect pure returns on our investments, we need to also safeguard ourselves from lost direction. As I write to you, our world is in a state of unprecedented peril.

The hunger for justice is as strong as it's ever been and so is the threat to it. Unarmed black men seem to be the sole targets of those who have sworn to protect American citizens. Our government has thrown out bipartisanship and replaced it with more pointed fingers.

COVID-19 has been a ferocious force that has refused to be tamed with more confirmed cases than cured ones. Prominent televangelists have "cursed it at the root," yet it still continues to grow. We bless what it cursed and attempt to curse what it blessed. (Did you get that?)

With millions upon millions of unemployed Americans and people around the globe, we have been pushed without warning into a pandemic unlike any in our lifetime. With face masks and meteoric media reminders to practice social distancing, our world has been altered in ways previously unimaginable. And it is in this state of unrest that the church has been blindsided by problems as it feasted on comforts and pleasure. We named it. We claimed it. We spoke it into existence without the capacity to contain the overflow. We wore it. We rode in it. We felt the intoxicating stroke of the ego and rubbed shoulders with the bigwigs of life.

We were invited to the red carpet and strutted without a care in the world. What happened to us? I'll tell you what happened: We started looking down. We took our attention off of the One and began to gaze at temporal pleasures. I enjoy my share of earthly benefits, yet heaven is always on my mind. We stopped looking up during a time we needed to do just that the most.

I feel as if we are frantically trying to regain our footing and attempting to grasp a time that once was. The world ran out before us to rescue humanity from its woes. We are stuck playing catch-up when we created the track on which we are to run!

If you are one of the fortunate ones in the body of Christ, I salute you as a worthy soldier. Yet if you find yourself waning in your confidence in God, I encourage you to lift your eyes! Here we see Jesus—our Chief Example—considering the power of the Everlasting Father on a fallen creation destined to hell forever. He didn't lift His eyes for His own sake. He did it for us.

I count this as the first step to building lasting friendships and relationships both inside and outside of the church. It's when we take our eyes off of ourselves that the real learning begins. It happens when we want to know how our fellow brother or sister is doing. How does life affect them? What makes them hurt? And do any lingering traumatic tendencies from the past plague them?

My ancestors were brought to these shores with a dexterous iron hand that only released its grip to clench more victims. We were stripped of our heritage. A legacy burned and a kingdom tarnished, we produced more and more in our likeness. Yet the one thing that remained was our spiritual identity. The Ethiopian eunuch in Acts 8:34-39 was miraculously saved. The Bible says he "went on his way rejoicing" (NIV). Whatever moves us emotionally usually prompts a verbal response.

I can see this prominent Ethiopian traveling to indigenous tribes and cultures telling them what the Savior accomplished on Calvary. I imagine him baptizing and laying hands on leaders, commanding them to be filled with the Spirit! This gospel was preached to African people by disciples who were inspired by the apostles, yet were manipulated by white colonizers into embracing a whitewashed, idolized version of what their ancestors believed.

How can the winds of this pain not blow down on successive generations? Yet through it all, we still believe! Thanks be to God for those who stood up to atrocities and unfair treatment! I applaud every soul who has kept their eyes "looking unto Jesus" (Hebrews 12:2, KJV).

A good start to unity and reconciliation is following the perfect example set by our King.

We must look at our world with uplifted eyes.

GROUP DISCUSSION QUESTIONS

Do you feel racial division keeps us from looking up to God for answers? If so, why?

How do we take our eyes off of ourselves to learn from others?

Do you feel the church's main focus is geared more toward financial blessings or spiritual ones? Why or why not?

NOTES

_____

_____

_____

_____

_____

_____

_____

_____

_____

_____

_____

_____

_____

_____

_____

_____

_____

_____

_____

_____

CHAPTER 2

THE DIVINE GIFT

One of the most humiliating aspects of being black in America is the blatant rejection we face—in one way or another—daily. Take a look at the judicial system and how imbalanced it is towards African Americans, brown people, and many other peoples of color. There's the clutch of the purse as we walk by white ladies in department stores and the lack of professionalism and respect when we attempt to make transactions deemed "too expensive." We also deal with the "You're not as smart or important as I am no matter what you've accomplished" bravado. Who wants to make friends with people who feel they are better than you? These attacks weaken the immune system of love, and any attempt at reconciliation is going to be challenged. I'm not ignorant of this truth.

Some people determine Black America's worth holistically on the premise of if they *feel* we are worth something or not. We are measured

21

by our work, the size of our name, the call on our life, and the culture factor. It's not based on fairness—or even sovereignty for that matter. We are a people worldwide who in many ways are governed by our appearance. It is one of the reasons some rapidly transform their demeanor when others are in their company.

Social media—at times—gives an impression that we are within arm's reach and ear shot of our worth and value, yet the opposite outcome is usually found.

The fatherless ponder their worth. The insecure relish the opportunity to escape their condition. Money can't wash off how we truly see ourselves. Success won't either. We can become victims of our states of mind that are formulated by the opinions of people we will never meet!

So you see, if it's true that in John 17:6 the Father wrapped each one of us up as a shiny package to present to His Son, it would be in our best interest to see what this "worth thing" is all about. Let me be clear. We are not objects; we are human beings who develop by our natural and spiritual experiences.

As with leadership, we need someone to follow. We need a motivator who encourages us in our deepest despair as we face our tallest mountains. I've lived long enough to know that other people's opinions will never help shape my image; they will only mar it.

Jesus said in John 17:6, "I have revealed you to those whom you gave me out of the world. They were yours; you gave them to me and they have obeyed your word." And it was Jesus who came in the name of His Father to fulfill a righteous passion (John 5:43).

It was this same Jesus that placed His divine words between us and our difficulties to shield us from a life of pity and self-wallowing. He came to provide purpose! I say all of this to say, how dare any man or woman purposely attempt to devalue what the Bible has called a "gift!"

Every soul has been handcrafted by God, yet throughout history, many have seen it differently. It was Carl Linnaeus, a biological scientist of the 18th century, who created the taxonomic (organism classification) system that led to how we classify different races of humans.

Google this man. He described the entire black race as cunning, lazy, lustful, careless, and a host of other insulting adjectives. I'm pretty sure you know how this story ends with Mr. Linnaeus crowing that his own people group was superior. It is assumptions held and assertions made such as these—by those seated in places of power—that can leave a large crowd of followers persuaded.

Who are we to even attempt to curse what God has blessed? When has it ever been right to label and assault the credibility of an innocent people? As those who bear the name of Christ, we have been given to Him. This is an indisputable fact. We have been called out to do great exploits, and no force can stop that as long as we believe it. I believe Jesus prayed for me. And it is my belief that causes this petition to work for me here on earth.

It is His mighty intercession that actively rests between me and my adversity. With Him, I win every time. The basis of my confidence is the revelation of the Father given to me. The Gift Giver gifts the gift. Go figure. The pain frequently carried is now untraceable because my worth has been handed to me by God through Jesus.

I am worth something because the Father said so. I am more than a statistic because of the blood of Jesus. I have unbroken fellowship with God through the finished work of Calvary! Hallelujah! I've always belonged to God and so have you, yet at the fall, our memories were wiped. We forgot where we came from, so we hitchhiked on the road of life until the first car pulled up and told us we were headed in the right direction. We opened our ears and heart to the driver without vetting their words.

In John 17:6 we see something completely different! A creation with a resting place, given by the One who gives rest, so that we may fight against the restlessness of living life with a skewed identity.

Just as we cannot love others if we don't love ourselves, we cannot fathom making peace with our enemies until we make peace with our God. We can say it's the "other group" all we want, but discovering how loved we are will be the catalyst for a reconciled heart.

THE STORM

January 6, 2021, forever changed our nation. American terrorists stormed our historically respected Capitol with the sole purpose of overturning the results of a settled election. I was stunned as I looked at this large group of white rioters as it looted, harassed, and demanded justice.

Never in my life had I imagined witnessing such a scene. Almost equally appalling was the lack of police presence to de-escalate the mob. Many Americans rushed to their phones to report their feelings on this monumental attack on democracy.

Some compared the police presence that is strikingly different at Black Lives Matter protests to the much friendlier approach on this day. There was no way to argue this fact.

We went silent from the shock of this event. It was horrifying. Just as my white friends in the past initiated conversations with me on why black people were so upset with law enforcement and the justice system in America, this day prompted me to seek answers for myself.

I was annoyed as responses rolled in one by one, "I'm not the one you should ask about this." Or, the four-worded response: "Yeah, it's a shame." Frustrated, I thought to myself, *Oh, now we're going silent? Yet I'm asked to speak when it's coming from black people.*

This disproportionate amount of empathy and respect needs to cease if we are ever going to get anywhere on this issue. When will we accept that in some way we are all crazy to some extent and have similar emotions?

Jesus did not suffer unto death so that we could suffer to communicate. His sacrifice provided the solution. I know everyone won't listen to what I'm saying, yet I do believe by faith that many will. Life is a precious gift, and we should value others as we do ourselves.

This tenacious act of kindness comes from the Holy Ghost living inside of a person. In our own strength, we can produce love yet not sustain it. God's love in unconditional and time is a condition. Think about that. We need a power that this world cannot provide.

The divine gift I speak of is His love for us and His stamp of identity on hearts that trust Him. Stand in line and receive yours today!

GROUP DISCUSSION QUESTIONS

What does it feel like to be rejected because of your skin color?

How does the gift of the Holy Spirit help make peace between lifelong tribal enemies?

What helps to shape us into the image of God? What mars His image in our lives?

How would we treat others if we saw them as gifts?

How does the lack of love for ourselves affect our relationships with those around us?

NOTES

_____
_____
_____
_____
_____
_____
_____
_____
_____
_____
_____
_____
_____
_____
_____
_____
_____
_____

CHAPTER 3

FREE SHIPPING

I love making online purchases. I get lost in the excitement of antici-
pating another toy to step on in the middle of the night. Or maybe it's
how fast items can arrive at my door with little effort on my part.

I'm a huge fan of technology; in many ways it makes our lives more
convenient. But what I believe I like best about online ordering is the free
shipping. It's the reward I receive for doing business with a company.

It's simple. I pick up my phone. Select the app. Order the merchandise.
In days, it's either at my door or in my mailbox. The problem comes
when I no longer value what's been purchased. When my child outgrows
the doll. When the nose clipper breaks again outside of the warranty
(true story). This is when technology fails me.

Jesus said in John 17:8 (NIV), "For I gave them the words you gave me and they accepted them. They knew with certainty that I came from you, and they believed that you sent me."

Wow! Talk about a delivered package! The Father used advanced shipping to get information to the Son, and the Son conveyed these words to His apostles free of charge!

Just think of how many words in the New Testament provide clear instructions on how to love God and our neighbors. Did you know that God wants us to love our neighbors as we love ourselves? (Matthew 19:19)

Did you know He wants us to love unconditionally? Did you also know that there will come a day when every knee will bow and every tongue will confess that Jesus is Lord to the glory of the Father? (Philippians 2:10-11)

It was at the expense of a spotless Lamb that revelation stood on a firm foundation. It was this mighty Name revealed to men that has provided a clear vision of who the Father is! I believe Jesus gave the disciples His Word in a variety of ways. We'll discuss two of them.

VERBAL DELIVERY

Jesus spoke on many occasions about the glory of God and the self-righteousness of the Pharisees who felt they dwelled in it. Jesus rebuked Peter and told His mother, while He was hanging on the cross, "Woman, behold, your son." Jesus faced zero interruption when delivering the good news of an eternal kingdom that burst onto the earthly scene yet could only be accessed through faith.

When Jesus spoke, things died and dried up. They also came back to life. When He said, "It is finished," it would never be resumed. Jesus communicated on a level that none had reached either before or has reached since His ascension into glory.

He is unmatched in every communicative way imaginable. He is the undisputed Orator of all history, and there will be no successor to His reign.

Jesus could talk.

SILENT DELIVERY

Another way I believe Jesus communicated with the disciples, who later became apostles, was through all of the messages He taught by silence. Stay with me because I'm taking you somewhere spiritual to influence what is natural. Think of Jesus' first thirty years on earth; we don't hear much about those. Remember, He was the "Word made flesh." His actions. His zeal. His mannerisms. His integrity. His love. His fire. His hater (Herod)—all—confirmed that this was the most important, powerful, intellectual, loving, and perfect human being ever!

I say all of this to say to you that if Jesus lowered Himself and communicated in many different ways to make connections and do the Father's will, what do you think keeps us from lowering ourselves in our own estimation for unity's sake? Did you know that after we are reconciled to a God we cannot see it is outwardly expressed and confirmed in an unexplainable love and respect for those whom we can see?

I don't care how rich and powerful or educated a child of God is, they can only show fruit according to the tree that is planted. We throw up our hands with chaos and confusion, but what we lack in these moments is real power. The words of Jesus encourage us to get filled with the Spirit by speaking in tongues as the early church did. We nest in our biases and prejudices because they never challenge us to change. They only cheer us on to stay in our hatred.

Some will say, "Well, I'm not Jesus," but miss the scripture that refers to us as His ambassadors on earth (2 Corinthians 5:20). It annoys me greatly at times when I hear people say to me, "I don't know what to do!" If we have been given Jesus' words by way of the apostles, the guidebook does just that. It guides! What did it cost us to obtain it? What did we lose to gain it? If we would be truly honest with ourselves, when we came to Jesus it was because we wanted to rid ourselves of the worst part of us only to find out there was nothing that could be salvaged.

Our sin had to die, and He forever lives in us, thereby taking our place. Sounds costly on His end yet free to us. Why hold on to racial hostility when all things have been made new? Sure, we relinquish levels of our dignity at moments of sacrifice. We lose friends and loved ones, or maybe we never had the bond we thought we did? For me, I would go through all of the agony of my "mini Calvary" to be a representative of the One who openly represented my life on the hill of Golgotha.

Unity is bloody. Salvation is bloody. Reconciliation is a free gift sent to our door that we walk past, ignore, throw into the junk closet of our homes, or even worse, return to the Sender. The time has come to appreciate what has been given at someone else's expense. The words of Jesus are all we need to course correct and bring healing.

Receive them today by faith.

GROUP DISCUSSION QUESTIONS

What prevents us from loving others unconditionally?

What actions show that we love our neighbors as ourselves?

How will you use the words of Jesus to bring healing?

In what ways can we lower ourselves and communicate with people different than us?

How can we apply the words of Jesus to our broken world?

NOTES

CHAPTER 4

YOU'VE BEEN PRAYED FOR!
(I PRAY FOR THEM)

It was in 2010 that I was introduced to a prayer movement unlike anything I'd seen before. In this praying culture lies a belief that when we wait on God in a room, petition night and day, we get results. Time was the prerequisite—not faith. I was mainly an onlooker during many of these meetings and watched as white men told us what to pray, how to pray, and when to pray.

My blood began to boil as "intercession" was sent up before God as "incense" that then President Barack Obama would have his faith "perfected." Yep. It still upsets me years later.

What I also found insulting was people from a group historically known for mistreating and policing other cultures was now attempting to tell God what to do with America's first black President. In my opinion, it was racism of the highest order.

I've encountered many forms of racism in church. I can recall a time I stood on stage after a service with a family member and approached the pastor just to say hello. I remember him giving us an awkward glance and appearing to be overcome with a reluctance to speak.

I had never seen him do this with other groups, so the moment really spoke for itself. I also remember how I was only asked to perform music—playing into another stereotype that all blacks are good for is entertaining. I didn't mind using my gift, and we created fun moments, yet the blatant disrespect to someone who has much, much more to offer proved to me that racism is alive and well in church.

From un-extended dinner invitations to "Hey, how many are you taking?" at the after-service refreshment table, if you can name it, I've probably seen it. My logic regarding it is that most people fear what they don't understand. They seek to tear down anything that may be perceived as a threat to the status quo.

I've seen black men with white wives given more clout in the church's hierarchy, while black families were kept at arm's length.

I've sat in small groups during times of mass shootings by white men and not heard a peep. It was like they hadn't happened. Yet, when Ferguson broke out in riots in 2014, it was all anyone heard about.

I've stood dumbfounded in many services as prayers exclusively for police officers guilty of having abused their power were hurled up to heaven. Not a word was mentioned about the gunned-down victims' families. Prayer is for all people. Plain and simple.

The hypocrisy. The arrogance.

Racism in the church is the most dishonest, hypocrisy-laden sin that we could ever commit. A soul that is filled with light and darkness at the same time has its light canceled out by the darkness it carries.

The fundamental question in our Christian life is this: Do you love Me? This question has been answered decade after decade from the lips of many parishioners yet lived out by only a handful. It's easy to say with lips of clay something we should say. It's easier to formulate words of reconciliation yet not implement plans of reconciliation—and I mean to God first and foremost!

It was during this time in the early 2010s that the Lord began to show me how pretentious many of our actions were. He allowed it to reach my emotions. I was hurt by the blatant disrespect for myself and black people. I wanted answers that I waited years to learn. What helped me greatly was not these futuristic revelations, not even close.

What helped me was a trip down Memory Lane to a place where the Son of God demonstrated the true intercession model by praying for me well before I was shaped in my mother's womb! It is this aspect of Jesus' prayer in John 17 that I want to focus on: the fact that we have all been prayed for by Jesus.

Unlike the bigoted leaders who paraded around church with spotted garments, making up stories and praying with iron canopies over their heads each time they uttered a word, Jesus was a Man who got what He wanted when He prayed. There is not one request that Jesus prayed for that He did not receive. Jesus gets what He wants!

The soon-to-be apostles received divine intercession to stay together as a unified body, to accomplish great feats in the name of Jesus, to give the church His words, and to turn the world upside down! With the exception of Mark leaving Paul and Paul opposing Peter's hypocrisy and racist behavior, there isn't any solid evidence this team broke up. They disagreed and argued, but what kept them joined was the prayer of none other than Jesus Christ!

Jesus strategically and specifically talked to the Father on behalf of these multidimensional world shakers. His prayer got the results He wanted. This truth grants me peace and joy because it reveals to me that Jesus wanted to pray, knew how to pray, and had a flawless connection with heaven! Imagine having a prayer life so accurate that results manifest each time you prayed. Wow! I'm not sure I even have the capacity to know what that would feel like.

What I do know is this: Jesus praying for you is far better than what any man can ever do! The model He set in place is worth practicing in our lives. True connection occurs between us when we pray using the words of Jesus.

Instead, pious preachers sprint ahead of the Word and make more messes to be cleaned up. They do more harm than good. Many of them present doctrines of devils to large numbers of followers, doing the work of their father the devil.

Even if we use our own words to bring healing and harmony, they are not powerful enough to create a sustainable solution. Some problems that were here before we got here will be here when we are gone. It will take a Word that was here before we were, is active on the earth today, and will be here well after us.

"I pray for them," in John 17:9, is specific. It is unique. It pinpoints purpose, and it expects desired results. I embrace this glorious confidence in the center of my being. If I would pray and believe it's already done before a thought hits my mind, I would believe that the word of unity and peace with God and my brothers and sisters in Christ is active in this realm. I would expect miracles to manifest!

There's one word I would use if a person asked me what it would take for the church to be unified, but it wouldn't be a word of my choosing. It would be a name of my choosing. That name is Jesus. Miracles are in that name! Love is in that name! Peace is in that name! Joy is in that name! Purpose is in that name! Power is in that name!

Jesus includes those who love Him in this prayer as well when He says in John 17:20: "My prayer is not for them alone. I pray also for those who will believe in me through their message."

To those of us who have been Spirit-filled, we cannot break up! Why? Because we have been prayed for. The deception comes when we are tricked into believing we are separate! No more excuses of why brotherly love can't continue. We have an Intercessor who loves us!

Thank you, Jesus! I've been prayed for! And so have you!

NOTES

_____

_____

_____

_____

_____

_____

_____

_____

_____

_____

_____

_____

_____

_____

_____

_____

_____

_____

_____

_____

CHAPTER 5

NOPE, NOT YOU (I DON'T PRAY FOR THE WORLD)

The title of this chapter may come off as brash or rude. To others, it may be shocking. However, now that we know who has been prayed for, our focus needs to shift to whom Jesus has *not* prayed for.

Yes, you heard it right. Jesus specifically prayed for those who would believe in Him through the words of His apostles. It seems kind of harsh. I know.

Let's go further into this thought. Returning to John 17:9 (NIV), Jesus prays to the Father these words: "I pray for them. I am not praying for the world, but for those you have given me, for they are yours."

Why would God, who loved the world so much, only accept intercession from His Son on behalf of twelve men who inspired the early church to be a thorn in the side of Greco-Roman society?

EXCLUSIVE

One thing we need to understand to be able to answer a question like this is the exclusivity of these hand-picked disciples. Jesus promoted each one to fulfill a specific role. Each had a personal encounter with Jesus. Most of them saw Him face-to-face, heard His cries and screams of agony from the cross, and consoled His grief-stricken mother. They witnessed innumerable miracles and saw the masses following Him everywhere He went. They noticed how He went around doing only good and healing all who were oppressed, for God was with Him (Acts 10:38).

The apostles were a special group of men touched by God to be vessels of honor, pouring the oil of God on those who believed. They were the wise master builders of the church (1 Corinthians 10:13).

They were Christ's ambassadors on the earth who inspired others as they unwaveringly moved in signs, miracles, and wonders.

It makes perfect sense why Jesus would pray for them. It makes equally good sense He would pray for those that would believe on Him through what they said of Him. What is not clear is the focus of God.

A WORLD IGNORED BUT ENCOURAGED

The Bible says in Psalms 9:17 (KJV) that "The wicked shall be turned into hell and all the nations that forget God."

The word "wicked" means "to be morally corrupt." We don't hear it much anymore, but morality equals heaven. Point blank. There is not one of us who can live upright 24/7. Not one. The word "nation" here in this scripture deals with ethnic groups. This means that any group of people—no matter its earthly merits—will perish eternally without faith in the apostles' words, given by Jesus. This scripture is also letting us know that those who practice immoral behavior will be permanently moved to a place of eternal unrest.

It is my belief that when God calls us out on our sin as we walk with Him, it is our obligation to leave it behind. So even His children walk a narrow path into the city that has neither night nor need for the sun to give it light (Revelation 21:23).

Ask yourself this question: Do I find myself struggling with a Messiah who sweated drops of blood in the Garden of Gethsemane from all of the weight of sin (past, present, and future) for every soul ever on earth, yet who prays such a tight prayer for a fraction of those He loved? Why would the gospel need to be preached until the end comes if there were no threat of an eternal resting place *not* called heaven? Why would He agonize to a point of distress that the human frame had never carried before or has carried since?

Logic of the basic sort should scream back to us that we were in deep trouble and needed a Savior. That's the gospel. This is the essence of reconciliation. That a flawed creation was destined for the grave and after that eternally perishing souls. It's frightening.

I believe the world was died for—but not prayed for. This scripture confirms my position. Jesus is not subject to our terms. His opinions can't be swayed or manipulated. We cannot pay Him off. He is Lord. He is God! He was "God with us," living a perfect life in corruptible flesh.

He ignored our demands that we keep our lifestyles just as they were when we answered the call. He rejected our righteousness to replace it with a right standing of His own. So tell me: Why would racial injustice remain an anchor in your belief system? Why are you so passionate about a world that is going to soon pass away?

What is it that makes you believe that America is the first item on God's bucket list? Is it because of our land's Founding Fathers who tickled the ears of this nation's citizens? Was it two-faced slave owners who proclaimed salvation for whites and condemnation for blacks? Or is it because you see your people group frequently in the public eye, and it makes you feel good to know that "God shed His grace on thee" . . . and turned His face from me?

What is it? I want to know! I'm using my anger correctly by asking questions. White brothers and sisters, tell me—why is nationalism more important than kingdom dominion? The powers of the nations are fading away. Jesus said they would. Perhaps it's why He prayed like He did. I ask of the nations this question: Why hold on to a world that is eroding day by day? Come out of the world and into His marvelous light! Give Him your nation, and let His wonders unfold in and through you.

If we are going to make it into heaven, it's going to take more than only being reconciled to God. It will take a love for the nations because that is the only outward expression that heaven sheds its light on.

"I don't pray for the world." This quote posted on Twitter today would rock the earth with controversy. Jesus cared nothing about that. He's not the God of renovation; He's the God of "all things have become new" (2 Corinthians 5:17, KJV).

If you really want to walk in the fullness of reconciliation (one with God, one with man), you need to toss out the idea of the world's view of the nations. It's more united outwardly than the church, yet more lost. I say we are lost because of our distorted view of what it means to be "one."

Our view of one is based on our relationships. It's based on our economic brackets. It's based on our occupations and giftings. It's based on what we look like and how well we live. It's based on every temporary pleasure that the world fights passionately to control and perpetuate, yet our minds are veiled from the truth.

We only unite if we have a connection with God that is opposite of what the world says it should be. We are only as connected to each other as we are to God. Always remember, the world has diversity, the church has reconciliation! I pray that in our lifetime a broader brush will be used to paint a picture of unity that heaven can smile upon.

Reconciliation is much deeper than diversity because we who were once God's enemies have now obtained His favor! We now have access to the resources of heaven to love Him first and also our neighbors! We have been given His Spirit to interact with His children on a much deeper level than just sitting next to each other in church and working together.

If we are going to grasp the depth of reconciliation the Bible talks about, we must ask the Holy Spirit to change our thinking and to open our lives to each other. Our ministries, churches, families, and businesses will reflect this divine swap!

If it is fought against this hard, it must be incredible! Reconciliation blows past fellowship; fellowship is the language of the reconciled. Reconciliation is the sign that peace has been made between long-standing enemies. I'm convinced this is a miracle. It's when we see the desire to pursue love with others that we know peace is present.

I'll admit that it will take more than a handful of committed followers to influence change, yet change is imminent. We must move beyond just talking about it. We must get to a place of action. Action requires effort. God stripped Himself of His heavenly royalty to save you and me. Purposeful. Powerful. It will take similar humility from each of us if we are to ever see the "one"—the oneness—Jesus so passionately desires.

Sorry world. You can't have that. The church can, but you cannot.

GROUP DISCUSSION QUESTIONS

Why do you feel Jesus only prayed for the disciples and the church?

What does reconciliation look like to our generation?

How do we communicate the gospel in such a hostile day?

What is the difference between reconciliation and fellowship?

In what ways do you feel the church can be better at showing true unity?

How can peace be maintained between those who were once enemies?

What actions will you take to make oneness a reality—in your heart, family, relationships, city, state, country?

NOTES

CHAPTER 6

LINK UP!
(THAT THEY MAY BE ONE)

That brings us to the crux of this book. Oneness is the *pièce de résistance* of God's plan. One with Him. One with each other. Many of us are accepting of peace with God yet devoid of a close, tangible connection with our brothers and sisters who are Christians like we are.

The Bible clearly states in 1 John 4:21 (KJV), "And this commandment have we from him, That he who loveth God love his brother also." This is a commandment. A commandment is a law. It is an order—not a suggestion. I've seen so many pastors throughout the years who had a deeply profound love for those who were far away from them, yet they felt coldness towards those they considered their nemeses. In many ways, I feel like the Christian life for some is lots and lots of busy work.

We look occupied, but there really is no depth of roots down into what God has charged each of us to do.

White pastors participated in chattel slavery and thousands of lynchings during the Jim Crow era. It was white leaders who laughed, mocked, scarred families for decades, and never looked back at their wicked deeds. If you've read the Bible before, you know that it is full of characters. Some obeyed like Joseph and David, while others like Saul and Ahab did not follow in the ways of the Lord.

It was white America of old who sat at the dinner table around 5 o'clock in the evening, folded their hands and prayed to God to bless the food while screams of terror, cracks of whips, blasts of shotguns and wails of toddlers for their mommas echoed in the background. They sat there and passed the buttered rolls around the table as they overheard black wives pleading with slave owners to let their husbands live. They overheard the din of death many nights, yet still they maintained (in their minds) unbroken fellowship with heaven!

Many white men's wives awakened in the middle of the night to a cold side of the bed where their husbands should have been sleeping. Instead, their husbands (some pastors) groped, molested, raped, and tortured beautiful black women they ostracized in society when the sun was up, but met face-to-face when the sun was down. (Some of our black women are faced with similar treatment in society today. It's not right. Black women are just as much God's creation as any other people!)

Imagine the embarrassment—or acceptance—of the woman who shared her husband's matrimonial privileges with a slave. I'm not sure what she felt. Maybe, just maybe, some of these women, as they lay in their beds, cried out to God for the Lord to come. Maybe they got down on their knees and pleaded with the God of Abraham, Isaac, and Jacob. Perhaps their pain and loneliness led them to sow seeds of righteousness.

I believe it was because of betrayal in many homes that intercession for unity finally broke out. It is laughable that we are expected to look at America through the same lens as white Americans. There are too many traumatic experiences historically for this to ever happen. Too much pain, loss, and hurt. There is a White America and a Black one. The disproportionate levels of power and influence evidenced between the two is enough to make any person want to throw up their hands in disgust.

OUR PROBLEM

One of the problems we have in America is we have a past no one wants to look back at! It's like a car without any rear-view accessories. Ours is a "keep both eyes ahead" country.

Why is that? I ask on this platform because I can't get a straight answer on other platforms. Is it normal? Is it abnormal? Is it guilt? Is it pride? Is it our unhealthy craving for power or our need to prove we are better than another group? Is it because we feel the ills of the past have no lingering consequences? Do we think it isn't our responsibility to think back to a time before our birth?

I'm running a pulse check to isolate the issue. I'm up late thinking about the root cause of this situation. I'm finished blaming a devil who's under our feet. This is in our power to fix!

Choices of the past create opportunities for the future. Violence of the past can find its way into future generations. Don't fall prey to the "It wasn't me" mindset. It will only produce spectator behavior. It has already weakened us. It continues to betray our ancestors willingly. It is gaslighting an entire generation and manipulating the masses. We're broken—fragmented. We are destitute, and the majority accepts it.

BUT JESUS PRAYED!

Did Jesus pray that the nation would become one, or was it His church? If your answer is no for the nation but yes for the church, my follow-up question is this: When do you think He wanted it?

Think about it: He prayed that the apostles would receive the Word and share it. They did that. He prayed they wouldn't break up. They didn't. He prayed for the church on earth and not the world's decaying system. He got it.

I began this book by stating that the person I can trust wholeheartedly to get a prayer through every time would be Jesus! I said that what He wants, He gets. Every time.

Yet when it comes to being one as a church, Dr. Martin Luther King Jr. once said, "It is appalling that the most segregated hour of Christian America is eleven o'clock on Sunday morning." He would still be appalled today.

Even in this megachurch age when people travel for miles and miles to hear their favorite speaker, we still have a tendency in metropolitan areas to keep our distance. What is ironic about it is the church—you know, the one that is always above sin, the one that constantly puts down the world for all of its ungodliness and idol worship, the one that is the "head and not the tail" and "above and not beneath," the one that "lends but doesn't borrow"—is found wanting and needy.

I've said before that diversity is not unity. If our attempts for unity stop at the door of diversity, we are left with nothing more than optics. Perhaps I'm being too hard on us, but what frustrates me is we've had more than two thousand years to fix this problem, and it yet lingers.

We should all take responsibility. It's on all of us.

If Jesus prayed and got everything else on His list, why not this? Is oneness among redeemed people groups too much to ask for? Is it the fall of man that leaves it hanging in the balance? What is it?

My belief is that we have oneness but the enemy has deceived the church for centuries that we don't have it. He has stolen our faith in this area and we see the ripple effects in our day. The "god of this world" has power to blind men and women's minds from the truth (2 Corinthians 4:4). If the church walks in the flesh, the fruit will be a mind of flesh blinded in the same manner. Jesus sewed it in His prayer in John 17. We have it! And it's our time to break down the walls that keep us divided!

I believe that previous generations sowed reconciliation, and now it's time to reap it! My generation refuses to let this chance pass by us. It's going to happen! Jesus' prayer, active on the earth for centuries, and His Word confirms it. Reconciliation is available because Jesus made it so.

Tough conversations must be had with the goal in mind to fix what is broken. Integration can take place as it did during the sixties but with great awareness centered around real oneness. One—meaning one only with God—is not true oneness unless it is expressed in our daily lives. If we love God, it must be evident in the way we love His children.

LINK UP!

So link up. White pastor, link up with your nemesis. Black pastor, link up with your enemy. I also speak to the various ethnic groups in America—now is the time! Our world is in danger. Fear is prevalent, and the only hope we have is Jesus. No longer be selfish; don't sit back while throwing up your hands saying, "I don't know what you're going through."

Enough of sympathy without empathy. Sympathy says, "Too bad for them." Empathy says, "Too bad for us." We need to rid ourselves of our carnal nature and seek to bring healing. Pastors, I say to you under the anointing of God, make sure you have the Holy Ghost like the Bible instructs. Be concerned that your followers possess it. Preach it. Teach it. Be accountable. Stop making excuses for your weakness, and just get into the presence of God.

Repent for your wrongs, and open your heart to what God says is right. That's going to be uncomfortable because your daughter may bring home a man who is not of your people group. Your son may fall in love with someone who doesn't speak English well. Some will have precious little mixed children and multiethnic in-laws.

Jesus, in His prayer in John 17:21 (NIV), asked that "all of them may be one, Father, just as you are in me and I am in you. May they also be in us so that the world may believe that you have sent me." Jesus was so intertwined with the Father that you couldn't tell them apart—the Father, the Spirit, the Son, the humanity. He was God in the flesh who dwelled among us! We beheld the wonder of His glory, the only begotten of the Father full of grace and truth (John 1:14).

He was God enough to say, "Before Abraham was, I AM "(John 8:58). He was man enough to say, "I thirst" (John 19:28). Jesus was God's revelation of oneness between man and Himself. Jesus was God's expression of Himself. Jesus was and is our Star Example on display for eternity.

We don't want to look at a union this deep. We don't want a relationship with God that is this close. You know how I know? I know it by the way we treat one another. I know it by the hardness of our hearts. I know our tree by the fruit it bears. I know we are lost after being found when we ignore the need to fellowship with our neighbor.

Neighbor: the one nearest to you. Do you know how many international ministries US churches sponsor? Yet how many INNERnational ministries? What I mean by that is how many organizations on these shores do we have that love their neighbors who are so close to them it's as if they were them! We are more concerned at times with the way things appear and less concerned about the way things actually are.

How can a person willingly ignore another person who constantly obstructs their view? Day after day, year after year, decade after decade, century after century? We teach unity from the pulpit as a buzz word but go home divided. Our behavior is hypocritical, and we need to fix that. No matter how many ways you present this problem or how eloquent or thought-out the path may be. People still ignore it and walk in blindness. We need a real view of what oneness is. It's not a denomination. It's a state of unbroken fellowship between God and man for eternity!

However, Church, reconciliation with God is not enough. We need more—much more. Let's take action.

GROUP DISCUSSION QUESTIONS

What is oneness with God?

What is oneness with man?

What is the number one thing that hinders oneness with God and man?

What is repentance?

How does repentance relate to oneness?

NOTES

CHAPTER 7

SANCTIFY THEM

Have you ever heard someone say, "I'm saved, sanctified, and filled with the Holy Ghost"? What does that even mean? Isn't that what my grandmama said when she was dancing around at church? Isn't that for old people?

In John 17:17 (NIV), Jesus prayed, "Sanctify them by the truth; your word is truth." I believe many people are uncertain of what Jesus meant when He prayed that we would be sanctified. We're going to take a look at what sanctification is, why it's important, and how we cannot live a life devoted to God without it.

SANCTIFIED!
You don't see this written on t-shirts! I think I have probably seen just about every other kingdom phrase on a shirt except this one.

The Bible definition of sanctify is to render or acknowledge, or to be respected or honored as holy. Sanctified things were separate from profane things and dedicated to God. Sanctified people were purified eternally by renewing of the soul.

How can a person who is born again by truth (Remember that the truth is how we are sanctified—how we are set free from bondage.) live a disrespectful life? And before you tell me I'm forgetting that we have a human nature that we call "the flesh," I'm including the flesh in my questioning.

Isn't that the reason we need salvation? Don't we need to be torn away from our sinful nature and joined to the divine nature? This is the essence of the faith we profess.

If truth sets us free and separates us from sin, why do we continue to walk in it? To me, the easiest definition of a person being sanctified is a person set apart for God's special use.

For years we have shied away from this word because it is transformative. It is the environment a soul that is truly born again experiences once it is saved. I'm not talking about that "in-and-out" version of being saved—the person who is saved Sunday through Wednesday, in bondage Thursday and Friday, and lost on Saturday! That's not a respectable way to live. No one desires that quality of life.

As with anything in life, there is a learning curve. It takes years to walk in holiness, and the flesh is still there to tempt us! But what separates a soul to be used by God repeatedly at a high level and not sporadically is a life that is completely yielded to God.

NO STRINGS ATTACHED

Sometimes in life when a person gives someone a gift, it comes with hidden expectations. This leaves the recipient of the gift blindsided once the favor is asked to be returned. God doesn't give like that! When He saves us, He saves us. He readily, speedily forgives any person who has committed any act. He frees them and places them at the table with Him forever!

The problem comes from our end. We are not as generous as the Living God. We make a decision, and when it doesn't appear to be rewarding, we quit. We sign up because we heard about the blessings of God and how they would overtake our lives. Who wouldn't want that? Yet, after God sets us aside for His use, He begins a process of making us the honorable, purified little ones He expects to exist on earth.

Critics will rant, "Nonsense! Once you're saved, that's it! It's a finished work! You can't earn anything! It's all by God's grace!" My rebuttal to that is simple: Why then does Jesus specifically pray for His apostles and for any who would believe Him through their words to be set apart? Why were they left in the world if God expected nothing of them but to meander their way through life?

Sanctification is direction! It tells us how to live—what to avoid—and compels us to love. Jesus prayed like this because He knew the flesh would rise up within the disciples (and us) to hate a holy life. He predetermined our steps on a road to heaven because that's where sanctification leads. When we are sanctified, the drugs go away. When we are set apart, the lust is destroyed. When we are driven by the Holy Spirit to produce the fruits of the Spirit, we see lasting results!

It is my belief that the truth can expel all forms of fornication from our hearts. He can erase all of our pride. We have heard countless stories of people who had terrible drug habits, heard truth one night, and were forever changed! But look what stayed behind stubbornly.

The sin of racial prejudice is one of the most powerful forms of hatred that exists. Why do we make such a giant out of something truth can easily step over? I have never heard in my twenty-three years of being saved a testimony of deliverance from racial biases. I have never had a person come up to me and ask me to pray that they would be freed from racism. I would have so much compassion and respect because I know that God doesn't want this disease in His set-aside ones!

What if God is holding back your influence until you turn over this problem to Him? You continue to fight it and say no, but He won't relent. You wanted to be "saved," and He wants to save all of you. Sanctification is a soul that is all-in! Salvation without sanctification is like lungs without oxygen. It's like a home with no foundation. I sigh heavily in my heart during moments when people who say they love God show they are not committed like Jesus wants them to be. It's hurtful to God.

THE SOLUTION

If we are ever going to get to the place of being separated from profane (impure) things and dedicated to holiness, a belief must form once conversion comes. In 2008, God came to me one morning as I was studying a lesson titled: "Race and Reconciliation," by Greg Howse and Michael Posey. The topic stood out to me unusually at the time. Up until this point in my life, the only churches I had ever known were black churches. It's culture. It was the church standard I'd seen at that time in my life.

When I was five years old, Mom was being abused by her husband, so she moved my little brother and me to Minnesota to stay with in-laws. It was during this time we eventually moved to the city of Eagan, Minnesota, which at that time was 99.99999 percent white. It was through abuse that God birthed a desire in my heart to learn about our lifelong enemy: white Americans. Growing up I never saw white people visit any of my family members' homes, and here I was in 2008 thinking back to my experiences growing up in Minnesota. *Why me?* was beating like a drum in my heart.

"I want you to start walking in reconciliation. I want you to join churches that are different from you. I will be with you and bless you. Tell them about racial reconciliation."

What?! I exclaimed in my heart. *No, I don't want any part of that!* I didn't want it because I knew God was asking me to suffer for His name's sake. I knew there would be people who didn't want us around. I knew some would play up to stereotypes and prejudice. All I thought about were the negatives, there wasn't much room for positives.

Yet I never knew how much He would use me and how many friends I would encounter. So many of them I still remain in connection with until this day. So many life lessons I learned and fun times we shared.

What came to me in 2008 was truth. For over the past decade, I've been associated with whites on a spiritual level—way different from what I grew up experiencing in my childhood. God set me apart before He made the world for this work. He made me to be a bridge but not the kind that gets run all over. He wants me to be a strong bridge, a wise bridge, a bridge that challenges all sides. This bridge has more than four lanes. It has collaborative roads that wind and bend—each of them leading straight to the Father.

God, in His divine foreknowledge, knew I would need to step out from what was familiar to uncharted waters for someone with family background. I allowed His hand to uproot my life to plant me into the hostile ground historically occupied by those from a different tribe. It was there that I flourished! Many times God wants us to step out from people and places we are accustomed to so that we can break away from influences that are hurtful and hindering. This is another example of sanctification.

Of course I gave in. I gave God my normal. I was all-in, set apart and uncomfortable being so. My kids were brought up in a predominantly white church. Meeting various ethnic groups, my life has changed a lot since the day He approached me. He has developed me and challenged me and many others to love, and it is still a work in progress. Idols take time to fall. I've been able to align with who He called me to be due to Jesus' prayer in John 17.

He used truth to block me off from ungodly pleasures and desires and demanded me to love. From that day, reconciliation has consumed me. I named my ministry after it (MOR—Meetings of Reconciliation). I've been asked to speak at events because of it. I've proclaimed it from stages using my cultural art form (rap). I have made paintings about it, developed friendships from it, and inspired thousands of people to—at the very least—consider walking in it.

So I say with great confidence again that when Jesus prays, He gets what He wants! If you're fighting, you won't win. Give in just as our Savior gave up His will in the garden for a cause not His own. What are you willing to lose? What are you afraid to gain? God gave to us with no strings. He wants the same from us. Give in. Live right. Love hard. And pray earnestly! Your destiny is full of people who are not like you. Learn that down here before it shocks you up there.

Be sanctified!

GROUP DISCUSSION QUESTIONS

What are you willing to give up that God's purpose may be fulfilled?

Have you ever branched out from your people group to learn about a people not your own? If so, how was this experience?

What do you feel sanctification means for our generation?

Have you started on the ministry God told you to start? If no, what is holding you back?

Are you confident that God will raise up people who will be bridges of unity and reconciliation?

NOTES

CHAPTER 8

NOTHING BUT THE TRUTH (YOUR WORD IS TRUTH)

Black Lives Matter!" yelled the multiethnic crowd of peaceful protestors as they defiantly marched through the streets of the metropolitan city. "All Lives Matter!" yelled a large group of conservative voters—also multiethnic.

The conservative group was locked arm in arm on the sidewalk; its mass stretched a block and a half. As the BLM protesters passed along, their chant overshadowed the ALM unit's attempts to be heard first. Moments of tension—to say the least—simmered between both parties.

With the sound of rubber bullets bouncing off parked vehicles and the stench of tear gas filling the air, pandemonium ensued as each group frantically scampered to find relief from iron-fisted law enforcement officers stressed out from long shifts and a tarnished image.

As chaos proceeded, muffled chants from behind partially covered faces (due to the COVID-19 blocking face masks) continued from high rise apartments. What a mess!

This is a quick review of 2020—a year many want to forget. With Twitter flooded with vicious tweets from our then Commander-in-Chief and the majority of the nation's rebuttals against these messages, our world was and still is hemorrhaging. It's still looking for something.

Truth. That's what each group wants. Whether it's rich white people telling the African American community to "get over the past" and to "quit looking back," or frustrated blacks who feel there is much going on right now necessitating everyone to look back, we must solve the race issue in our world and the economic imbalance that crowds our globe. Looking for relief from the hands of men is like attempting to solve world hunger on a budget.

Society has always connected the most with negative behaviors and experiences. They're what get the blood pumping and the adrenaline flowing. What's a water-cooler moment without some good gossip? What is life without drama? These thought patterns have a tendency to plague our lives and leave us broken and searching for truth.

THE TALK

One day a ministry friend reached out to me wanting clarity on a post I had made about the conditions of the church during racial moments in our country's history. I had challenged every white person whom I had worshiped with throughout the years—some who are now my friends—to be there when friendship was needed the most.

The deaths of George Floyd, Breonna Taylor, Ahmaud Arbery and countless—and I mean countless—others reached a fever pitch in my mind, and many of my white friends did not seem to care. I wanted to know how they really felt about not only my family and me, but my people as a whole. Many responded, while others chose to keep silent. My hurting heart wanted truth.

As I spoke with my ministry friend who was twice my age and had cut his teeth as a police officer in the early sixties, I could hear he was dismissive of the plight or "struggle" African Americans rich and poor alike suffer in our country. As we talked, I mentioned facts, not out of bitterness; I spoke the truth unapologetically. I stated fact, after fact, after fact attempting to stir his empathy—to no avail. "Slavery is something you know nothing of!" said the perturbed senior.

My pushback was that I wasn't there, but I can see its effects today. The disproportionate amounts of wealth alone between whites and blacks is a red enough flag for me that says, "Something is wrong here." The difference between us is dollars and opportunity. No one can convince me otherwise. In fact, the entire economic system has been constructed to discourage blacks from ownership.

Today, we don't see any "No Blacks Allowed" signs boldly attached to the entrances of stores, schools, neighborhoods, organizations or churches. That's because it is now an unwritten rule that manifests itself via price tags, credit scores, voter affiliation, group association and even doctrinal stances.

What disappointed me about my friend was that the truth did not seem to matter to him. He suffered from what I believe to be cognitive dissonance (mental discord). His privilege was an opaque wall between him and reality.

Jesus prayed in John 17:17, "Sanctify them by the truth; your word is truth." He was praying to God, "Lord, keep your children out of bitterness, rage, anger, hatred, jealousy, racism, greed, lust, and oppression. Do so by Your word. It is Truth." I believe thoughts such as these were in the mind of Christ as He petitioned our Heavenly Father.

TRUTH: A BIBLICAL DEFINITION

Truth is supposed to be objective. It describes an idea that is in accordance with reality under all considerations. This is the biblical definition for truth. We don't want to hear it, but God's justice is objective. He loves the unjust judge as much as He loves the persistent widow (Luke 18).

God is patient and will not be swayed by our imperfect definitions. He will judge saints and sinners alike—not by their deeds but by His Word. God's Word produces. God's Word convicts. God's Word creates dry ground in wet places and pools of water in the desert. It transforms dry bones into strong armies full of life and vigor!

His Word is sharp because it's always active. It doesn't rest because eternity is imminent. His Word frees those in bondage and quickens a discouraged preacher's confidence. As our words are containers of power, how much more so are those of the One who formed the universe—all using His words. No contract, His Word is the contract! If His Word can limit waters of the sea, He can limit the hatred in our souls.

I wrote this book for people who want to see reconciliation in our lifetime! Until our hearts receive the conditioning for truth, we will continue to deny facts that to our brothers and sisters of color are self-evident. We will continue to betray and hurt one another. We will find ourselves in a perpetual state of bitterness and brokenness.

Your truth—or even mine—doesn't matter. His Word does! God's Word is the answer for every problem we've created. My prayer is that you allow Him to mold you more into His identity. That your heart would become soft and sensitive. That the oil would flow in your families. That hatred would no longer be a temptation you yield to.

When Jesus prayed this most powerful prayer, He released truth into the universe that has the capability to set men and women free! Use your faith to unite—not separate. Use the Word of God to find direction—not give it. Develop eyes for the one and not just the ninety-nine. Quit ignoring books of the Bible that challenge you. Let your eyes be released from arrogance (Proverbs 6:17).

Reconciliation with God and man is the only way a soul can be eternally peaceful and satisfied. Let truth redeem your losses. Repent and see His wonders! It's going to take miracles to bring the church together as one. It will take leaders walking in truth to gain the respect and attention of a newly ascended generation.

God prayed that we would be set apart by truth. Are you?

GROUP DISCUSSION QUESTIONS

What does truth mean to you?

Why do you feel so many people challenge truth?

What holds you back from following God's Word?

What is the number one thing that you feel blinds people's eyes to the truth about racial discrimination and prejudice?

How can you speak the truth on this issue in love?

NOTES

_____

_____

_____

_____

_____

_____

_____

_____

_____

_____

_____

_____

_____

_____

_____

_____

_____

_____

CHAPTER 9

THE FACT PACK (FOR THOSE WHO WILL BELIEVE)

It is truly sensational what can happen if people would only believe. I grew up in a home with low expectations. That fact certainly made higher expectations seem like a pipe dream.

Life my way, we just wanted to live to see another day. We were survivors. You were rich if you had all of your utilities on, a car to get to work, and the latest fashions to wear. We believed in God but questioned if God believed in us. If He did, why was life this way?

As I get older, I see the importance of maintaining a strong belief in God. We need His covering, and we need the heavens opened over our heads in order to see His power in our lives. This is where the battle is staged—in our minds—the battle for trust in God. This battle spares no one. Every bishop, prophet, evangelist, teacher, leader, and elder who has ever lived has waged war in this attack for his or her confidence. The Bible calls it the "Fight of Faith" (1 Timothy 6:12).

What I love about God is He doesn't allow His children to fend for themselves. He helps us. But we must believe that we are helped. We must believe that Jesus has already done the heavy lifting. He did so by using His Son to install presets of power in our walk with Him that bring forth healing, deliverance, wisdom, grace, authority, and abundance. We simply must be willing to tap into the Source.

Revisiting John 17:20, I want to focus on Jesus' words: "I pray also for those who will believe in me. . . ." In this passage, we are witnessing the perfect foreknowledge of God that He used to form the earth and universe. This established the next phase: the inauguration of the church. What foresight! What wisdom! If we would only grasp the truth of this moment, it would truly re-energize our faith for today.

See, you and I are similar. Don't think for a moment that I don't understand pain and the fight against my faith in God. My life has been full of troubles and death-defying escapes that would make any daredevil envious. I've been so low in life that I questioned who I was and what my purpose was. I felt I was nothing but a burden to my mother, having been born to her and my father at age sixteen.

So, if you had come to me when I was a troubled teen and said to me that God had prayed for me long ago, I would have had some colorful words to share with you. Why? Because I believed I was living in hell with predetermined levels of subpar expectations set for me.

You can ask any black person—for the most part—what America's expectations are for black men's lifespans, and you may receive even more colorful words. They won't be your favorite color either.

Ask most black people if we celebrate the 4th of July for its true purpose and see what response comes back. I say this to get you to see the cognitive imbalance we as Americans have in our country when it comes to our expectations. We think different. It's factual.

If a police officer pulls up behind me, I'm not overcome with warm feelings. I feel uneasy, and my expectations need to be as reasonable as they can be in that moment because we all know how dark these encounters have the potential of becoming.

I believe we must learn to manage our emotions and expectations. I'm learning to depend on God to make everything what it needs to be. I'm learning that joy is a safeguard against the lofty expectations of my soul.

I'm unsure if I expect our country to become better. I'm almost certain things will grow worse. I place my belief in the act of God praying for me before I got here. I have access to not only His power but to a lasting relationship—one that is beyond earthly things and also beyond death.

Jesus is real, if you didn't know it.

THE FACT PACK

In the 1960s, there was a group of rambunctious, flashy, affluent celebrity friends who formed a group on the Las Vegas Strip. This group featured Sammy Davis, Jr., Frank Sinatra, Dean Martin, Peter Lawford, and Joey Bishop. They referred to themselves as "The Rat Pack."

Way before my time, this iconic bunch formed a lifelong bond that was electrifying. They sang together, danced together, made movies, partied, partied, and then partied some more.

Google these men and you will see how much fun they had together. I'm sure they loved the ladies and how much money they made as a unit. Many would come along and attempt to recreate this legendary team but to no avail. It was a once-in-a-lifetime group.

They formed a bond that was encouraged by Hollywood. It was nurtured and maintained. Why can't we be like they were in the sense of being a bunch of radical, fired-up, focused, and determined people who have a bond formed by belief in the prayer of Jesus in John 17:20?

What would it look like to carry truth and belief in the same hand? Power and a testimony? Faith and a witness? Will we be remembered only for the Azusa Street Revival of the early 1900s, or will we plant our stake of reconciliation in our day? I believe we want it, but we don't know how to bring it about. I believe there's a bunch of believing Christians who have laid down their desires and expectations to see God's will be done!

The beauty of it all is we don't need to know how it will all play out; we just need to believe. To increase our faith day by day, all we need to do is treat our neighbors right. We can see a movement in our day unlike ever before. A movement where all cultures rest under divine culture. A movement where hatred is erased by the presence of God.

We need a place where His glory resides. We need to plan for it. We need to join together as one, with facts from heaven. That new life truly comes! That joy is attainable. That peace is possible.

Intercessors need to unite from a kingdom perspective and not let our differences divide us. There is a level we can all reach, but it's only by prayer, proactiveness, and perseverance. Heaven has given us all the facts we will ever need.

"For those who will believe" is evidence! Dictionary.com defines the word "fact" as "something that has actual existence." Jesus exists! His church exists! Reconciliation exists! Hope exists! Belief in this day and age is a fact. There will be many who will believe; Scripture proves it!

My question to you is this: Are you in that pack? If your answer is yes, just know that you have been prayed for by Jesus, and He will sustain your desire to believe. Our faith will be challenged on many occasions, yet it is our belief that never leaves us—all because of a prayer made in a garden by a Savior two thousand plus years ago. Remarkable!

In the end, life will play out the way God intends, for we know the battle is not ours; it's the Lord's (2 Chronicles 20:15). Make sure you are on the winning side.

GROUP DISCUSSION QUESTIONS

Do you have a diverse group of friends with whom you can share your thoughts about faith?

If you are the only person from your ethnic group in your circle of friends, how does that impact you?

How important is it to pursue relationships with others who see life differently than you do?

How do you handle unbelief?

NOTES

CHAPTER 10

IS HE THERE? (AND I IN THEM)

As we near the end of *One Is Not One*, I want to be sure of your connection with God. Some of my statements may have shocked or angered you. I know that each culture has its own set of beliefs and principles that shape its traditions. We are all made from one blood; however, our experiences vary.

I wrote this book to call to attention the division between whites and blacks and many other ethnic groups in God's vineyard. I know we can talk to each other. I believe we can love each other. We just need to understand how important that is right now. It's time for real discussions—no more sugar-coated conversations.

The difficulties I've witnessed, the adverse circumstances African Americans have endured time after time after time are not who we are! They are what we have had the unfortunate opportunity to look at through the lens of long suffering. My black people, I did not write this book with only you in my heart, yet I highlighted our horrors only to shed light on a truth hidden for centuries.

Our stories are worth telling. Use your voice. Don't let others determine what should and should not be said. Don't take prejudice on any level. I promise you that the Lord will fight for you; you need only be still (Exodus 14:14).

I wrote this book for every person who bears or will bear the name of Christ. I wrote this book for bishops to cascade to their pastors, for senior pastors to gift to their associate pastors, for associate pastors to pass on to their leaders, for leaders to share with their volunteers, and lastly, for volunteers to model in their homes.

One can never truly be one without two factors. The first is being connected with God. The second is being connected to each other. I make a deposit into the body of Christ with the authority and permission God has granted. All who listen to the message of reconciliation in this book and implement it will have lasting results and overwhelming joy. I guarantee you that if you will grow your connection with God, enormous amounts of joy will flood your heart and fill the hearts of those around you with happiness.

It is our call as Christians to be ambassadors of Christ, to stand between heaven and earth asking God to turn ugly racial injustice and all other injustices around. To grant us the mindset to model heaven on earth—not just in our words but on our staffs, through our payrolls, and around our dinner tables. To love as He loves. To forgive as we have been forgiven.

Always remember: As goes the church, so goes the world.

Jesus utters four amazingly encouraging words in His prayer in John 17:23: "And I in them." We need more men and women, young and old, who are filled with the Holy Spirit like in the days of old! (Acts 2) We need unified Spirit-led people to disrupt the principalities that make people hate.

Racism is a spirit, and the only way to destroy it is with the blood, power, and authority of Jesus Christ. I find myself at the height of confidence when I think about what He is capable of! Time is drawing to a close. This world will soon be made new. Make sure you are ready!

God is raising up an army in these end times that will not be afraid to let Him reside in them. When God gets in us, we change! I know for some of you that challenges your comfort levels because you're so close to detrimental behaviors that you have learned growing up. It is time to be free! No more chains. No more sin. No more hatred.

I speak to the entire body of Christ when I say that true, biblical reconciliation only comes when we are right with God and right with our brothers and sisters. We are creatures who are dependent on close relationships that bring healing and trust. It's time to kick the devil out for good!

Reconciliation takes time, but it's past time to hit the start button. Let hell know that God is in you and that you will not be intimidated as a minister of reconciliation. Don't be satisfied with diversity. I pray you become bored with optics and appearances. I'm hoping millions of you will let go of doubt and fear to grab hold of peace and happiness.

So I ask you: Is He in you? If your answer is yes, how do you know? Is it the tears that fill your eyes as your favorite worship song comes on? Is it the way people speak well of you and admire you? Is it your gifts to the poor and your extensive Bible knowledge? Is it because of your visions from heaven and even your connection with angels? Is it the relationship you have with your pastor? Is it your credentialed background and degree-filled walls?

Is it your good heart and kind nature? Is it your vehemence for orphans and widows and the poor? Is it because of your illustrious entourage of friends? These are impressive earthly comforts, my friend, yet the best ways I know of that demonstrate you truly belong to God are the infilling of the Holy Spirit and the way that you love your brothers and sisters.

I know by the way you tolerate people you don't have to be around. I'll see it when you don't get your way and are cool with it, by the self-control you operate in when your views aren't accepted, and how you feel about the stranger. I know you have faith by your works. No person can show you their faith if they will not show you their works.

One is all we are in heaven. One with God. One with eternity. One with our glorified bodies. One with our new surroundings. One with the saints of old and the recently redeemed. One with life everlasting. One with the nations. Our ethnicities will still be intact, yet they will be seen as beauty and not boundary (Revelation 7:9).

This is God's definition of one. This is His standard of oneness. This is His challenge to us. This was His Son's intercession for us in the garden. This is the oil poured into our lamps to overflow onto those around us on earth. May it overflow onto heaven's crystal sea! Only through peace with God and our eternal family can one truly be one.

Your brother in Christ,

Dre Williams

GROUP DISCUSSION QUESTIONS

Why do you feel we will keep our ethnic identities in heaven?

What do you think unity looks like in heaven?

What does it mean to be one with believers here on earth?

NOTES

EPILOGUE

I hope *One Is Not One* has made you think. I pray your groups and churches are inspired to be that minister of reconciliation that the world needs right now. I feel many of the same emotions you do about what's going on. Some days it really shocks me how bad things are yet how unwilling we are to come together to fix our brokenness. This sort of message is fought by devils because they know how powerful unity is. Evil spirits work diligently to prevent us from coming together in this life.

This book reaches beyond the borders of my country—America. It reaches the shores of Africa, the land of my ancestors.

It reaches to Asia, Australia, Europe, Brazil, Canada, Mexico and every other region. This is a worldwide problem. If life ever pushes you to a place of discomfort, fight to stay there. It's the comforts of life that can fan us to sleep if we are not careful. Please remember your neighbors. Love them. Pray for them. Learn about them. Ask God for the insight, power, and grace it's going to take to do His will. And lastly, be brave. Push beyond the norm. Disrupt something. I thank you in advance.

ABOUT THE AUTHOR

Dre Williams is an author, speaker, teacher, and coach who is on a mission to see lives changed and purposes fulfilled using his God-given talents and abilities. With his crystal-clear and inspirational messages of perseverance, deliverance, and transformation, he is a sought-after keynote speaker and professional facilitator.

Dre is the founder of MOR (Meetings of Reconciliation). MOR is an anointed deliverance service that aims to destroy every work of the enemy.

In his first book titled *Dre Williams ... It's Already Done!* he takes you back to where it all started. Horribly abused and abandoned as a child, Dre paints a vivid picture in this encouraging, personal narrative. With a unique style of communication, he uses words to enwrap readers in what he wants you to feel.

It's Already Done! will leave your heart full of hope and encouragement to resolutely face your giants! Uniquely woven together are a powerful testimony, biblical insight, and practical perseverance. Dre teaches current and future leaders policy, leadership skills, and confidence training as a professional facilitator in the corporate world. Possessing a heart for leadership, he loves to share wisdom and knowledge to further the careers of diverse professionals.

Dre lives in Dallas, Texas, with his beautiful wife of twenty years, Llechor, and his precious daughters, DeYanni and Lauren.

Follow me!

Instagram: dre_will

Facebook: @theconfidentcoach

YouTube: lifeofdre